THE WRITINGS OF MARIAN A. YANCEY

A CREATIVE AUTOBIOGRAPHY OF MY WRITINGS THAT TOUCHES ON SOCIAL ISSUES AND SITUATIONS BASED UPON MY CULTURAL TRANSITION FROM RURAL TO URBAN AS AN AFRICAN AMERICAN FEMALE, EMPHASIZING SOCIAL AND SPIRITUAL GROWTH AND AWARENESS

MARIAN A. YANCEY

ISBN 979-8-88685-755-9 (paperback)
ISBN 979-8-88685-756-6 (digital)

Christian Faith Publishing
832 Park Avenue
Meadville, PA 16335
www.christianfaithpublishing.com

Printed in the United States of America

To my fallen warriors and ancestors in the struggle: Shareef Makail, Fuquan, Russell, Pooh, and Andre. My mother, Phyllis Yancey, and my father, Richard Yancey; my grandmothers Rosa D. Yancey and Callie Mae Haskins; my grandfather Jake Yancey; my favorite uncle Joe; and my brother, Russell Yancey (he was EXCELLENT). May all of you be resting in peace. In the holy name of JESUS.

Life before Newark, New Jersey

"Ma."

While browsing through the aisles of a Dollar General store, I came upon a special soap that indicated "no additives" and claimed to be 100 percent pure. The wrapping and the name of the soap caught my eye. It said, "Granma's Soap." This soap looked so familiar to me. I felt compelled to pick it up and smell it. The smell was so familiar. I am not a psychologist; however, that soap triggered loving memories of Ma, my grandmother Mrs. Rosa D. Yancey. It suddenly occurred to me that my grandmother used to make this soap in her kitchen on our farm in Buffalo Junction, Virginia. I read the ingredients which were mainly lye. Suddenly, I remembered that my grandmother called her soap "lye soap." Yes, this was the same soap. Only God knows how many times I was washed with that soap. I naturally carried the soap to the register and paid for it.

Later, after using the soap, I sadly remembered Ma; this was the special name for my grandmother who had raised me from a baby. My parents had moved to New Jersey when I was a baby in search of work. Rumor has it that my grandmother wanted to keep me. This was during a period in history called the "northern migration." This was a period when numerous African Americans left the south in search of work and a better life in the north, escaping oppression and Jim Crow in the south. The saying "It's the little things in life that count" is true. This commercial version of my grandmother's homemade soap triggered a level of comfort for me as I lovingly remembered "Ma." This soap thoroughly cleaned my body and my spirit. Amen.

The last time that I saw Ma alive was on the back porch on a fall afternoon. I had just gotten home from school. Ma was ironing, and suddenly, she gasped, and exclaimed, "Oh!" She then grabbed her chest quickly and stopped ironing. Suddenly, Aunt Willie came out and told Ma to lie down. As usual, I followed Ma into the bedroom where she lay. She whispered to me, "Mar-un, make sure you keep the house clean." Those were her last words to me. The next day, I had planned on going to see Ma immediately after school. Sadly, she had passed while I was still in school. Aunt Willie met me at the mailbox in her car with the sad, sad news. The pain that I felt was unbearable. This was October 13, 1971. I was thirteen years old.

"Look, Russell, a rainbow!" I shouted loudly to the brother whose face held an innocent, enchanted look. I quickly pointed ahead of us, and then we both ran as fast as we could to follow the soft, pastel colors. Russell and I both loved chasing the rainbow. We really did think we could find the end of those rainbows we loved so much. We were very young and unblemished back then. Russell was five, and I was six. Life in the country was such fun! We both loved sun showers because we knew that soon afterward, a rainbow would appear.

Russell and I would run to find the pot of gold at the end of the rainbow. We never did find it. Life in the country was simple and carefree. We climbed trees. We played in the dirt. We weeded tobacco plants for our uncle Kite. We worked in the garden with our grandmother Ma. Life was beautiful and innocent growing up in the country. Funny, life had a way of changing things. We grew up, and the colors of the rainbows faded.

Gray took over the shades of pink and blue. Life changed, and we were lost in a fog of confusion. This is what happened to Russell and me. After Ma passed, we went to live with our parents in Newark, New Jersey, in October 1971. I was thirteen, and Russell was twelve. We had to adjust to our new living environment. We were given nicknames by the kids on the block. Russell's was "Country," mine was "White Girl." Unfortunately, Russell tried hard to fit in and developed a drug addiction in the seventh grade. I couldn't fit in so I stayed in my room and wrote.

TRYING TO ADJUST TO LIVING IN NEWARK, NEW JERSEY

Sitting in my room, I write…

Hope

Shadows fall
But day is breaking

clouds gather about
in marshmallow shapes
clumped together in a crowd

—a bird sings

harsh winds blow from the east and the west

rain falls
lightning strikes

—but day is breaking
A bird sings

ANNIVERSARY SONG

Sky's turning deeper blue
as it dances across my mind
you are the stallion grazing alone
I am the sea

With its changing waves
YOU are like the sun as it
rises over the mountain
I am the pricked finger
you are the bloody rose

Lying down on wet grass
closing my eyes, remembering
how we danced all night
holding one another close and
wishing time away
felt how your eyes blazed deep
like midnight into my soul

Sky's turning deeper, deeper blue
as it dances across my mind
you are the stallion grazing alone
I am the crashing sea
with its seagulls flying overhead

You are like the sun as it shines
brightly into the day
I am the pricked finger
you are the bloody rose

Crying dewdrops on the hot sand
closing my mind trying not
to remember
how we danced all night long
holding one another close
wishing time away
feeling your eyes blazing deep
into my soul
I am the pricked finger

you are the bloody rose

HAIKUS

Say he is a bird
who once gently passed me by
to fly westward-bound…

here, sitting alone
with memories passin' through
bidding me hello…

though, you won't call me
I will still be sittin' by
hoping that you will…

A Rap Session

Hey, people, what's happening?
what?
no! you can't mean that
you trying to tell me that
nothing is happening?
listen, I'll tell you what
just look around and tell me what you see
what?
you still don't see anything?
oh, man!
this whole world is stuck-up
I guess I'd better get you together
No, you mean that you can't see death?

Listen, just take a deep breath
now do you understand what I mean?

look at the ground, is it even halfway clean?
now listen, meet me right here tomorrow and don't be late.
we still have to rap about hate.

FRIENDS

hey! don't turn your back on me
please! I need someone who I can turn to
so I won't feel so blue

hey! don't put me down
because I'm not sure that I
can get off the ground

what? all right! get lost!
who needs you!

THE DREAM

each night as I go to sleep
I pray to God that our love
will keep
and then I gently go to sleep
secretly smiling to myself
but as morning arrives
it's a different story
I wake up and look to heaven above
with tears in my eyes…
you see, I have no love

DANGER ZONE

once upon a time
I met an old man
and all at once
I felt so grand
he told me how to go to the outer limits
to the danger zone
but it didn't work
because I'm still alone

FOREVER

remember when we first met?
and everything was together
and you always said that this would be forever
but the days
they went fast
and I was so sure that it would last
but that was the past
you see, nothing is forever

I Remember

I remember when we were
always together
I remember our first kiss
in that moment of bliss
I remember when you said, "I love you"
I remember when I said, "I love you too"
I remember all these things
because this is all that I have left of you.

CYCLE

the sun rises
the ocean splashes

and the seagulls fly
in that sky
of
blue
I really don't like to see these things
they remind me of you

QUESTION AND ANSWER

1
2
why am I so blue?
I know why
because there's you

Sorrow, My

my sorrow is so deep
(I feel as if the sky is caving in)

my sorrow is so deep
(I feel oh-so numb within)

my sorrow is so deep
(I have lost a loved one so dear)

my sorrow is so deep
(that my eyes cannot shed a tear)

my sorrow is so deep.

DESCRIPTION

free as a bird
untamed as a tiger
wild as a stallion
but as gentle as a pup
all these things are you
my love
and
more.

REMINISCING

here I sit with nothing to do…
thinking about the world and its problems
and you

I'm a Phony

so long
see ya
farewell
catch you later

Is this really what I want to say?

THAT'S AN ORDER!

enjoy these days of hope

cherish the moments in which you are gay

for they will not last long

and remember the old-school song
and the group that you belong

pray to God to let you not hate

this savage world of which you are draft bait

* * * * *

My dream man would have to be taller than I am and would have to be gentle, understanding, and fun to be with and not too serious. I guess there would have to be something about his looks that attract me.

We could meet at a roller-skating place like Twin City, and he probably would have to knock me down and help me up. Then, later on, he would ask me to skate. Later, we would get to know each other better then meet again the following week to skate. From there, who knows!

* * * * *

got no time for tears
got no time to let my feelings through
I came this far
can't afford to look back now

try and understand
follow the wind while
it's blowin' coldly against your skin
feel its presence
'cause baby it's there

got no time for pain
got no time to remember yesterday
I'm too close to my dreams
can't afford to look back now

try and understand
catch the sun
while its warmth is still inviting
feel its presence
'cause, baby, it's there.

Give a Toast

cheers!

to the good old days?
to the days of tomorrow

DENOUEMENT

—and thus, she stood, gazing
into her lover's eyes
eyes of stone: unfeeling, distant, and desolate…

—and thus, he stood, feeling the wasted vibrance of past life remembering her fire, her body, and feeling her eyes: warm and burning deep…

—and so they did each turn their backs to one another to walk away…tired…drained…remembering…

WILD STALLION

Wild stallion, blowing in the breeze
restless spirit, dancin' under glaring light
alive one
resting, moving
moving, resting
forever refreshment, stay just as you are

say you are the wind
say you are the soil of the earth
say you are the coolness of spring water
say you are joy to me
say you are pain
say I wouldn't have it any other way

wild stallion, growing wings
restless spirit, singin' praise

alive one, searching for truth
forever refreshment, vibrating emotions

say you are the wind
say you are the soil of the earth
say you are the coolness of spring water
say you are joy to me
say you are pain
say I wouldn't have it any other way

WHAT I CAN'T TOUCH

I see you
but I can't
reach you…
why?

How I See Myself

I see myself
as a piece of clay
I'm being molded

-N-

Shaped Into

something that I don't want to be… I yell
but no one hears…and suddenly, I'm hard

HOW I SEE MY NEIGHBORHOOD

In my neighborhood
I see hate, fear, ignorance, death, and waste
I see the cruelty of the world

THE WORLD OUTSIDE

the world outside can be good.
the world outside can be cruel.
it depends on how you look at it.

THE PAST

your eyes were always smiling—
happy were you

you never got tired of listening to me—
consoling were you

your hands were very gentle—
calm were you

but suddenly, I had to leave—

sad was I...

JUST LOOKING

I looked around
and there were your eyes locked into mine

I looked up
and your lips were smiling with mine

I looked down
and your feet were dancing to the same beat as mine

I looked in front of me
and you were all that I could see

That certain something

I wanted to reach out and caress you
but something held me back

and my eyes turned toward a distant view

I longed to talk to you and console
—but something held me back
I tried to fight it, but still, it said, "No"

I ached just to gaze into your secretive eyes—
but still that something held me back

then filled me up with stupid lies

Suddenly, I turned violent and tried to fight
—but that something held me back
and then you disappeared into the night

SIGHTSEEING

round and round
up and down
away I go!
don't stop…
I don't like reality

A PLEAD

love doesn't go
love doesn't walk away
love doesn't say goodbye
love waits…

QUESTION AND ANSWER

tomorrow—
what will it bring?
—who knows

LETTING GO

I thought I'd lost you
But suddenly, you came back

Only not for me
and then all at once, I felt so sad

I was so confused
that friends became strangers

the sky that was once blue turned gray
then the truth came out and swept me away

Though, I'll miss you very much
I'll have to let go of my dreams and that magical touch

IF

If I made you a magic carpet
that would fly at will
If I gave you all the riches in the world
If I get all the sweet-smelling things together and gave them to you
If I made your wishes come true
would I then
be worthy of your love?

How?

how can I die
without being afraid?
how can I live
without being afraid?

ONE WAY

he's looking this way
be cool
be cool
he's smiling this way
be cool
be cool

he's walking this way
be cool
be cool
he's running this way
be cool
be cool
he's passed this way
I'm a fool
I'm a fool

A Secret to Remember

sh-h-h-h-h
the end approaches
oh…
you know it

fondest wishes

good luck
happy-go-lucky, crazy, lazy, lovestruck you…
you'll need it

CONFUSED

You said that you'll never say goodbye
So why are you saying it?

HEY, LOVE

Hello, love,
how are you?
you know you are my love
just as there are stars
in heaven above

you know winters may come
-n- winters may go

but I just want you to know that my love will never

leave

DEDICATION TO A SUPERSTAR
(JERMAINE JACKSON)

so far away
are you
but all my hopes
will not turn blue
for how can I be sad over someone
I never had
but
destiny doesn't say
that we will never meet
and the happiness to come I shall greet
so for now,
I will sing, dance, laugh,
and let life

take its path

* * * * *

FYI. Years later, while working at the first-class ticket counter at Continental Airlines, I met Jackie Jackson, who is more attractive than his brother Jermaine. God is good!

THE WAY IT IS

After all this time
I see
for what I thought
can never be
I used to think
that we could work it out
but now I see different
for how can we lose love
when we never had it?

Can You?

Can you
tell me what's going on
so I won't feel so alone?

Can you get this world together
just like birds to a feather?

can you

renew the used—
I wish you could

so I won't be so confused

can you
do all these things?
because I just can't

A Desire

as the grains of sand
move gently along
come sit by me
and sing me a song
let it not be a joyful tune
instead make it a sad, moving one

as I gaze thoughtfully at the sun
sing it
and let your sweet voice float through my ears

down to my heart

wind-swept summers
dew-dipped, sweet blossoms

blooming into morning sun
that greets you in a saddened, yet sweet way

is that you?
are you existing
just for me?

wind-blown curtains
that sway to the natural rhythm
that says, "I'm here just to be."

is that you?
are you existing just for me?

star-dappled grass bent over from exhaustion
that grows only to be cut when it's grown too much…too fast…too soon

is that you?
are you existing just for me?

Come with me to the mountains m' love
rest with me while I think of tomorrow
cloudy skies covered with gray
sweet raindrops resting on leaves of happiness, past
shiny eyes, you're gonna miss me
when I'm gone

gonna miss my lovin'

when you're sleepin' and dreamin' of those cloudy skies
as my memory echoes deep within you
come to the mountains with me once more
rest with me while I think of tomorrow
and feeling those cloudy skies covered with gray
as the sweet raindrops rest on the leaves of happiness, past
stormy eyes, you're gonna miss me
when I'm gone

tryin' to reach that unreachable star
losing my pride
losing me
the sun glistens on the newly damp grass
hey, why am I wastin' mah time
there's so much that I have to do
so tell me once
let me know
love, are you worth it?

tryin' to reach that unreachable star
losing my pride
losing me
the sun glistens on the newly damp grass
hey, why am I wastin' mah time
there's so much that I need to do
so tell me once
let me know
love, are you worth it?

the rebel that you once were
the rebel in your soul
they've all gone to pasture
what happened to the eyes that held the light of day
when night had already fallen
the gleam that shined on and on
stand behind me…when darkness falls
the rebel that you once were
wouldn't let time pass him by
now time has gone
better vibes…better times seem to have all disappeared into the day
strawberry fields…blue skies
fly with the eagle searchin' for tomorrow as the rebel in you dies
as we fade into the day

we've walked through the shadows together, you and I.
passed through the various horizons that were laid out before us
we were confronted with the harsh awakening of reality
what could we have done?
we represented the innocent
the ones who longed for perfection
the ones who thought that there was a tomorrow

we've crawled over the mountaintop, you and I.
paused for a moment to review our life together
we each then stole a last magical glance at one another

who could we have blamed?
we were the lost,
the misunderstood

the ones who cried secretly among ourselves
the ones who thought that there was a tomorrow

we've knelt before one another, you and I
prayed that we may one day overcome our inhibitions
so that we may freely greet one another without regret or shame
could we have bravely begged-off yesterday in order to produce a
tomorrow
for us?

only, it seemed too late then
—for we were cast within the shadows of our remains becoming the
shadows of our own existence
we were the ones who shivered amongst the coldness
the ones whose eyes were blinded by the sun the ones who thought
that there was a tomorrow

love is pain…sorrow, knowing that we'll never feel the same way
about each other
knowing that there's no future

love is remembering the first meeting…the good times…the dreams
that are now dead, but still
stubbornly trying to come back to life

love is pain…sorrow, love is today's tears falling from your already-swol-
len red eyes, due to yesterday's
pain.

so long
why do you always
put me down

whenever your friends are around?
why do you always say, "I love you"
until you find someone new?
well, I don't know why
but this is goodbye.

An honest mistake

Hey, you! why are you
staring at me?
I'm not a freak from the circus or anything like that
what?
Oh, I'm sorry

Don't

don't say you love me
unless you do
don't kiss me
unless you want to
but don't leave me
I don't want you to

KNOWLEDGE

I should have known
from the way the twinkle in your eyes died
I should have known
from the way you smiled
I should have known
from the way you hanged your head
I should have known
but I didn't

RAMBLING

even though you're sitting
next to me
your mind is rambling
o'er the mountains, through the sky, and in the spur of a moment
It's with her

ETERNITY

when we were together
the days were too short
and the nights were too long
but now the days seem like years

TICKTOCK

although I only see you from a distance
although you never notice me
although your heart is with someone else
and although I try to tell my heart to stop, it won't

REMEMBRANCE OF ME

remember when you passed me by
remember when you said, "Hi"
but I think you were trying to prove something to yourself
if you don't remember these,
remember this—I'm not an old jar on a shelf

An open and closed case
the world opened up to me
when I saw thee
but now, it's closed.

OPERATION FREEZE

you're inside in the warmth

surrounded by your friends
and me
I'm outside in the cold…waiting

Sometimes, I wonder about you

where were you last night
where are you today
where will you be tomorrow… I wish I knew

EVEN

Even though you live close by
I feel that we are worlds apart
even when you say, "Hi"
I feel as though I should cry
even though I see you almost
all the time
I feel as though we're in a contest
even when you say, "Hi"
I feel as though, I shall die

A Quick Thought

while it's gently thundering

while it's quietly raining.
I think I'll remember you

MY LOVE

my love is handsome
my love is quiet
my love is gentle
my love he loves me
that's why he's my love

UNTITLED

'tis time to say goodbye, m' love
'tis time to say goodbye
alas, m' love
wipe the tears from your eyes
time, it seems to be on our side
on our side, m' love
'tis on our side
let us not be sad
fill this day with gaiety
with gaiety, m' love
fill it with gaiety

think o'er these words that are wise
think o'er these words
remember the valley that was
once green, m' love
the valley that once was green

oh, 'tis time to say goodbye, m' love
'tis time to say goodbye
alas, m' love
wipe away the tears flowing deep
time, it seems to be on our side
on our side, m' love
on our side

—and not knowing where I am
headed is to surely be unsure
not knowing what direction my life is taking
just following an unseen trail…letting the dust blind me

heart of my heat you pound eloquently within
love you for love
love you for now

—and not knowing where I'm going is surely to be daring
and willing to sit still
and laugh about old times

life of my life
our time is now
love you for you

love you for love

HAIKU

Say I am like grass
Although I bend, I bounce back
the bruise is still there

* * * * *

The opening was dark and moody. Its voice screamed quietly as I moved forward, awkwardly. I stopped, though, and turned around to walk away. I could not go in.

His eyes blazed deeply into her heart, making it pound harder and harder. She was amazed: Everything about his face proclaimed one emotion, anger. She was terrified. The tension in his face verified that fear. The unusual harsh lines around his mouth made his once spontaneous smile seem far away.

UNTITLED

wind-swept summers
dew-dipped sweet blossoms
blooming into the morning sun
that greets you in a saddened, yet sweet way

is that you?
are you existing
just for me?

wind-blown curtains
that sway to the natural rhythm

The cool, crisp, wind felt inviting as I stepped outside of that dark, stale house. The wind caressed my face and neck as it moved briskly westward. The grass swayed to the rhythm the wind made as it gently said, "Hello" and "Goodbye."

the time is now
—hello sad, blues day
can't seem to rid myself of you

thought that I'd never feel you again
the feeling's floating around
—hello blue, blue Monday
can't understand why you're always following me
thought that I could run away
the pain is now
—hello bad news day

can't escape you now
you've become a part
of me
sad, sad blues day
feelin' you
strong bad, bad news day

PHASES

we've been through some rough times together
you with your polished airs and well-established ways.
me with my fragmented mind. Driftin' in and out of space.
through all the old times
through all the new times
our lives consist of one
for all the old times
for all the good times
we'll stick together

we've become mellow throughout time and laughed in the rain
cried in the sun
you with your crooked smile
me with my dewy eyes
through all the old times

through all the new times
our lives consist of one
for all the old times
for all the good times
we'll feel on

we've been ripened with time
calmed down by the sea
we've crawled up that steep hill
you with your wise ways
me with new hope
through all the old times

through all the new times
our lives consist of one
for all the old times
for all the good times
we'll stay together

FLYIN'

he flew down from heaven, not long ago
flew down and touched my soul
sent me flyin' along with him
together we traveled side by side
just driftin' along
takin' our time
makin' it last
sittin' on marshmallow clouds
lettin' the sun make us warm
and lettin' the rain cool us

yeah, flew down from heaven, not long ago
flew down and touched my soul
sent me flyin' along with him

everything was ours, and we were everything
we laughed and gathered happiness while we could
tried to put it in a paper bag
But it turned into water and ran out
all too soon, he left
now, I'm just sittin' on the cold ground
takin' my time, remembering how he—

flew down from heaven, not so long ago
flew down and touched my soul
sent me flyin' along with him.

REALLY LIVING IN NEWARK, NEW JERSEY

I see myself as the defeated woman robbed of her dignity and stripped of past hope, dreams, future, and life…and love.

The tears, they flow freely, deep, and often.

My life consists of a set of strings dangling from a very blue space in time, each having its own select color and each swaying to a different rhythm created by the breeze from clouds passing by.

The ache, it persists, piercing deeper, harder, and constantly.

My joy has faded away, and I am left alone to face a tomorrow that is destined to come, filled with new hope and dreams…and new love.

Growing up in the '70s, I don't have to guess the difference in how people have changed their attitudes toward race, gender, and making money to now. The '70s was a time of extreme thinking. In my opinion, either you were very open-minded or extremely closed-minded. Now, everything seems to have taken on a different form. People don't express themselves as they used to, and the ones who do are labeled as liberals. Sadly, now no one is willing to become a martyr for their causes anymore. There are no more heroes. Yes, times have radically changed since the '70s. The mindset of race, gender, and making money has changed dramatically.

On the issue of race, in the '70s Black Americans became Afro-Americans. We began wearing our hair naturally and in a round and picked out hairstyle called the Afro. We shunned the oppressive ways of our captors. We were no longer Negro and colored. We were Black and proud of it. Black radical groups evolved, and they were definitely willing to die for the cause. This mindset started before I was old enough to appreciate it. Also, this was not *allowed* in Buffalo Junction, Virginia. However, I became a teenager in the early '70s in Newark, New Jersey. I was so confused because I didn't know if I wanted to become a hippie or a Black panther. There was so much diversity going on in the North. A teenager could become confused in the process.

I loved the hippie idealism. We had several on my block. I used to go over and talk to one of the ladies. We talked about natural beauty and being natural. I loved our conversations. The hippies were so open-minded and just wanted to love everybody. Race wasn't an issue to them. All colors were beautiful: white, black, yellow, red, brown, and whatever happened in the mix. It's too bad that people don't think like that anymore or at least try to think like that. The world would be a much better place, I believe, if the hippie revolution had not been terminated.

I was a young black girl living in the hood, and I wanted to become one. The hippies were beautiful people. The idea of making money has definitely changed. In the '70s, if you followed the hippie idealism, money was not a priority, and people were urged not to be materialist but spiritual. Money was often shunned and viewed as evil. Nowadays, it's all about the money. Morals and values have vanished for the love of money. IF only the hippies could have survived long enough to change the *establishment*, life would be better now. No more institutionalized social stratification. People would follow the law of God and love their fellow men. Treat your fellow men as you would like to be treated.

A DEDICATION

The sleep was a very peaceful sleep. There were colors of yellow and blue swirling around the insides of my weary mind. I dreamed of nothing that night but an empty colorful space. I remember how sweet my sleep was that deceitful night. The shaking began after I'd slipped into the color of blue. Yellow had floated away into a dark hole of time.

"Wake up! Wake up!" My daughter, Angel, yelled. "Shareef's been shot, and he's dead!"

Blue yanked itself from me, and I was left alone, trembling in icy darkness. I felt the coldness that only death could negotiate into my being.

My mind screamed, *Shareef can't be dead! He's okay!*

I numbly picked up the unwelcoming telephone and reluctantly dialed Betty's number. The persistent ringing of the phone only magnified my fears. After a great degree of time, Betty picked up the phone.

"Hello," she woefully exhaled.

I suddenly felt fear erupting within me, and I couldn't control myself any longer. I anxiously yelled into the phone as if I were lost within a cave. My voice echoed, "Is Shareef dead?"

Betty tearfully howled, "Yes!"

A spinning swirl of thick, black, gummy smoke viciously engulfed me, and once again, I was left alone in darkness.

I painfully visualized poor Shareef helplessly lying facedown on a warm, sticky carpet of crimson covering the cold, gray sidewalk. He was cruelly shot in the back. Yes, Shareef was dead, and there was nothing that anyone could do to change this horrendous truth. Shareef had valiantly honored death's chilly invitation to join him, and Shareef Makail was gone.

I sat at Betty's kitchen table later on during that dreary early morning vividly remembering the last time I saw Shareef alive. His death came on an early winter's morning, but I last remember seeing him in the vibrant sunshine of July earlier that year.

As I walked up the steps of 22 Brenner Street, Shareef was thoughtfully sitting on the third step down from the top of those old worn, broken bricks that lead everyone into the warmth of Betty's house. I remember being quietly happy that Shareef was seated firmly there. You see, until that time, I'd seen him only twice since he'd been home. I'd long moved away from Brenner Street, but it was still a part of me. Shareef had been unjustly locked away in prison for the past fifteen or sixteen years. It had been so many, many years since he'd been gone. I'd lost count. He'd told me a couple of years before his arrest that out of all the things he'd done in his life, he would probably go to jail for something that he didn't do, which is what happened. Shareef was charged with events that a friend of his did. However, the friend was killed before Shareef went to trial and wasn't alive to take the blame. So, Shareef was held accountable for his friend's crimes.

But never mind that, he was home on that hot day in July and the sun and God were happily shining down upon him. I remember asking him, "What's u-u-p, Shareef?"

Which was our common way of saying hello between us. Shareef vacantly looked up at me and slowly greeted me, "Hey, Marian."

I don't know exactly what was going through Shareef's mind at that time, but if you would ask any of his relatives or friends what did they think Shareef had on his mind at any given time, they would simply say, "I don't know." This is because Shareef always seemed to have a million and one thing was on his mind at one time. But he never talked about what they were. Nobody ever really knew what Shareef was actually thinking. It seems as if he was feeling his way around in the darkness as a blind man would who had no cane to assist him on his journey.

I then recalled how I'd seen one of his old running buddies at the mall a couple of weeks prior. I quickly stated, "Oh, I saw your friend, Shareef (another Shareef) at the mall, and I told him you were home. I hope you don't mind that I gave him your number. Did he call you yet?"

Shareef then flatly responded, "Naw, I don't even answer the phone unless I recognize the number. I'm trying to stay away from all that."

I then declared that I knew exactly what he was talking about. You see, Shareef was trying to desperately wipe his slate clean. He wanted to change. He wanted a second chance at life. To me, it seemed as if he was brilliantly succeeding at accomplishing this golden dream of a new life. He had at that time devoted himself openly to Allah. He had beat the odds of getting and maintaining a job with a criminal record. It seemed as if Shareef was holding his business down. I remember exhaling a mental sigh of relief as I said to myself, *Yeah, Shareef is going to make it. He's out of the streets, and I don't have to worry about him getting killed out there.*

You see, I was worried about Shareef when he first came home a year prior to that hot July afternoon. That day, I thought calmly to myself, *I don't have to worry about that happening to Shareef.* I quietly relished those thoughts of Shareef's safety as I cheerfully entered 22 Brenner Street, home of Shareef Makail Ali.

His mother, Betty, was sitting at the kitchen table in that cozy, friendly kitchen that all her guests and family always seemed to gravitate toward. No one hardly ever sat in the living room. There's nothing like sitting around that big, round wooden table with a nice, steamy hot cup of coffee offered by the hospitality of Betty. It could be a hundred degrees outside, but Betty and I stubbornly took slow, deliberate slurps from our cups of coffee. The coffee made the exchange of our thunderous thoughts more soothing. You see, Betty, Shareef, and the rest of the family are not my biological relatives, but I grew up around them and they are my people. They are my family, regardless. And that's that.

As with all the old dwellers of Brenner Street, we've known one another for so long that our spirits have entwined themselves together. We are one. We are an extension of one another. There lies a bond between us that cannot be broken. When one of us falls, we all fall. A part of us dies with that person. That's how deep our connection is to one another. Shareef Makail was not the first one of our brothers to depart from us on Brenner Street. The first one of my peers to embark on that journey of death was "Pooh." His unnatural death happened in December 1993. Shareef was killed in 2005. Pooh was shot down in front of 12 Brenner Street. His life was ripped away from us, and we all cried together. We sadly, relentlessly, and endlessly cry for Pooh still. All Pooh wanted to do was to get his old girlfriend, Lateefah, back and be happy—another dream terminated.

Another warrior to leave us was "Fuquan." I use the term *warrior* because it seems as if we were in a battle of survival on Brenner Street as are all other streets located within the shunned, hidden inner cities where poor, little black children grow up with lost dreams.

Jawanza Kunjufu, author of *Countering the Conspiracy to Destroy Black Boys* vols. 1 and 2, declares that since he's written his first book in 1982,

> The conspiracy has become worse. We have a greater number of African American males being placed in Special Education classes, dropping out of school, selling drugs, making babies, involved in criminal activities and being incarcerated. My greatest challenge comes from those who really don't care if Black boys grow into manhood. To that group I offer this observation: America spends 2,300 dollars per child to attend Headstart, and approximately 38,000 dollars per inmate to "attend" prison. The Republican administration chose to cut Headstart, a program that was shown to be cost effective, and increased expenditures to prisons which have an atrocious record of rehabilitation. Monies spent in Headstart for two years is far less than the lifetime allocations for prison.

In just the simple struggle of survival in the inner cities, many black men die. How far can a black man really go in a society that has hidden walls and glass ceilings, especially when he is born poor with minimal life chances?

Now, Fuquan was a tall, dark-skinned brother who used to look a lot like Jermaine Jackson back in the day. He had a severe stutter, which may have been one of the reasons he may have dropped out of school. Unfortunately, time was not kind to Fuquan. As he grew older, his long-term drug use withered his skin into a worn leather-like appearance. His teeth gradually, one by one, vanished into a void. His face became sunken as did his spirit. I remember walking up on Fuquan after he'd shot some heroin into his beckoning veins on the steps of my apartment complex. He was just sitting there looking as if he didn't want to live another day. It appeared as if all the dope in the world could not erase the pain that he was going through.

I quietly whispered to Fuquan, "It will get better, Fu!"

Fuquan woefully shook his head and flatly stated, "Not for me."

At that moment, it became obvious that Fuquan's long dream of becoming a professional boxer once again was long gone. At one time, Fuquan was famous for his one-punch knockouts in the ring and in the streets. Now, he faced his greatest defeat—life. I wish that I had argued more with Fu that day, but I was not as spiritually strong as I am now. I realize that anything is possible with God. You just have to believe. I wish that I could tell this to Fuquan now.

Fuquan was a strong black giant of a man. Yet the mask that he wore that day was the face of a man much older than he actually was. Still, Fuquan stood tall even at his lowest point in life. He still chuckled that crazy-sounding chuckle that that was Fuquan. He always had a joke and a laugh for everyone.

During this time, he was an intravenous drug user, and he had no home except for an old abandoned van parked in an empty lot. Fuquan was my friend. He was my brother. He left for eternity in the fall of the year 2000. His life was stolen quickly by another man's treacherous blow. He lost his life in a street fight. He's become sluggish from living on the streets and his continuous drug use. Fuquan was another dream terminated.

I remember a little boy named André. I remember sitting on the steps of my home on Brenner Street, watching little André go to the supermarket which was down the street with his mother. He was a cute, friendly little boy who wore black-framed glasses. Dré always had a smile on his face. I wonder what his secret dream was as he happily trailed behind his mother on their way to Foodtown. His dream, I never knew.

Dré became a young man on Brenner Street, and his reality ended on the side of 24 Brenner Street in the winter of 2002 by someone who was posing as his friend. Shot, Dré was left alone to painfully die in the snow in an open lot on Brenner Street. A little boy's smile faded into an endless void. Another dream terminated.

Sadly, I now sit at my own kitchen table, reliving all the cherished memories of my friends who once dwelled on Brenner Street. A melancholy mist of deep, deep purple envelopes my strength and cold-bloodedly captures my breath. I try to latch on to Shareef's, Pooh's, Fuquan's, and Dré's dreams for them. But selfishly, reality will not allow this to occur. So I stared beyond the obvious and engage my dreams for them toward heaven.

The late rapper, Tupac Shakur once questioned in one of his songs, "I wonder if heaven has a place for a 'G' like me?" Mercifully, the answer is "Yes."

I thankfully envision Shareef Makail, Pooh, Fuquan, and Dré all victoriously hanging out upon white cottony, fluffy clouds living out dreams beyond their greatest expectations.

I miss and love y'all,
Marian (White Girl)

Dear Professor Davis,

The last thing that I remembered that made me laugh was thinking about my brother, Russell (the aspiring lawyer and self-proclaimed advocate for the homeless). Before discovering that he wanted to become a lawyer, Russell was a lawsuit king. If somebody sneezed on Russell, he would try to sue them. Now I am afraid that Pandora's box has been opened since he started attending Rutgers University. He has devoted himself to suing everyone still. Only now he's representing himself. What makes it so crazy is that he's even won a couple of cases.

The latest case is the funniest to me because he's trying to sue City Hall, and everybody knows that "you can't sue City Hall." I was so sure that this old cliché wasn't just created on a whim. I was so sure of this. I even told this "advocate for the homeless" that you can't sue City Hall. I stated rather bluntly to him, "Russell, your a—— can't sue City Hall."

He then responded rather stubbornly, "Well, we'll just see about that."

Knowing how stubborn he can be, I then proceeded to tune his a—— out. Okay! Because Russell can be a very annoying person when he wants to be. He was just determined to annoy City Hall. He would go to the city council meetings and speak as often as they had meetings. He would begin his speech by stating, "Russell Yancey, here, advocate for the homeless." I'm pretty sure that the entire council started to clinch their teeth tightly together. Oh, he's been asked to leave the meetings several times. However, that didn't faze Russell Yancey, advocate for the homeless. Resistance only made him more determined and more annoying.

Last evening, Russell and I were sitting on the porch. He was talking, and I was acting as if I was listening. (I did this all the time, and trust me, he didn't notice.) Now I am ashamed of this. As long as Russell could talk, he was fine. I wish he could talk now. He thought everybody else was wrong and that he was right. I did catch the tail end of *his* conversation because he was reading a certified letter that he received from the city clerk. Russell exclaimed, "Oh my, they've dismissed my case because according to this act or title 56 something." It stated that City Hall had immunity against whatever he was suing them for. Anyway, to make a long story short—"You *really* can't sue City Hall!"

I thought this was so funny, and I laughed about it all last night into this morning. However, I'm sure that Russell Yancey, "advocate for the homeless," is working on his next case!

Sadly, I wrote this for one of the classes I was taking at Rutgers University before Russell passed away on January 18, 2009. He was caught up in a police chase on a Sunday afternoon after leaving church. The police were chasing a stolen car. It took me almost two years to finally get a police report because I was getting the runaround by the police department, particularly one Detective Nardone.

A councilman intervened and got the report for me. Russell's death was a cover-up. He was given an unauthorized autopsy just to confirm that he had a heart attack while driving. However, how do you explain the dents in his bumper that looked like the brackets that the police have on their cars? Unfortunately, I chose the wrong lawyer who bullshitted me and did nothing to help me prove what happened to Russell. He had a heart attack because he was afraid of being caught up in the police chase. You see, police chases were banned in Newark during that time. This was a cover-up.

At his memorial given by POP (People's Organization for Power), there were councilmen from City Hall in attendance. They presented a plaque in Russell's honor. There were representatives from Rutgers University and Essex County College. Rutgers founded a scholarship in Russell's name. Rutgers presented a posthumous degree to the family for Russell. He was due to graduate that semester. The *Star-Ledger* newspaper wrote an article about Russell. You see, Russell had overcome homelessness in the streets of Baltimore and heroin addiction. He was just realizing his full potential and was able to think clearly without addiction. He faithfully attended St. James AME church every Sunday. God can do anything. Russell would have made a great lawyer. REST IN PEACE, my sweet brother. Every time I see a rainbow, I will think of you. Another dream terminated.

And yet another sad, sad story.

I remember an older boy ringing doorbells and running anxiously up the flight of stairs to 105 West Kinney Street when I first moved there. It was Halloween, and he seemed to be enjoying himself. He was barely able to contain his excitement. I thought it was a little odd because he appeared to be too old to trick-or-treat. Now that I think about it, it may have been his first time trick-or-treating. He was the only one who came that night.

In that neighborhood, no child comes to ring your bell on Halloween. Instead, they go to the small stores up on High Street to get their candies. I learned this over the years that I lived at 105 West Kinney Street in University Courts. I was disillusioned that night because I had just moved there, and I thought it was a very nice complex. It still is compared to some areas in Newark. We had bushes and plenty of trees. The complex took up the whole square block between West Kinney Street and Court Street running alongside University and High Streets.

Years later, I still remember seeing this same enthusiastic boy sitting outside my window on a step of the building facing 107 West Kinney and sadly looking up at the third floor to an apartment window that he'd shared with his foster mother and two foster sisters. They weren't there anymore. That enthusiastic young boy had turned into a very sad young man. I will never ever forget the look on his face. The light behind his eyes was gone. There was no hope behind his eyes. I only saw raw pain as he sadly held his head up to look for ghosts of happier days. There is a song in church that tells God to "break my heart for what breaks your heart." My heart is broken for this sad young man.

His foster mother had passed a few years earlier. According to neighborhood gossip, the foster kids were split up. I am not sure of their ages. I am not sure if they had "aged out of the system." From the impression I received, Foster Care in Essex County, particularly Newark, Irvington, East Orange. Leaves a lot to be desired. This system breaks up homes, destroys children, and does more harm than good. It seems that *anyone* who needs extra income can get a child. This is dangerous. People get tired of the children and give them back. Children are taken away from the foster parents once they have bonded. It's horrible to me. Imagine the psychological damage that can happen to a child who is constantly going from home to home and just being snatched away once they become comfortable.

If God blesses me, I hope to start my own orphanage and give these children a real home—a stable home. They won't age out in my orphanage because they can always come home. I will have a follow-up program to assist them in adjusting to being independent and live in counselors. I have the whole idea in my head. All I know is that my children will get all the love, guidance, and protection I can give.

Now back to my story, I really don't know if the foster kids from 107 had aged out or not. However, I did hear what happened to one of them. After their foster mom passed, one of the girls was killed along with her boyfriend in their apartment. You see, if these kids had *aged out* of the system, they had to fend for themselves and go wherever they could find—food and shelter. I don't know what happened to this young man after I saw him sadly looking up at the third floor to 107. I never saw him again after that day. But I am sure that he was out fending for himself, seeking food and shelter whether it was in another foster home or on the streets, which, I fear, may be where he eventually ends up.

I pray for divine intervention in Jesus's name for him. I pray that he finds his way. I pray that he survived and is still alive. It's so sad to see a child grow up alone with the odds not on their side. May his dreams become true.

COLORS

Comfort is you
I feel as if I've found my way back home
you are a place
where darkness and light blend
into a peaceful gray…

I am one with you
you say all the right things
you make me feel the right way
I am suddenly wrapped up in a sky of yellow and blue…

your voice soothes me
your touch beckons me to come closer
and closer into you
you are the colors that I've been searching for…

I find myself riding on a swirl of gold, red, and orange…

PORTRAIT OF MYSELF

to be a freak in this society
of modern-day times
—tears and woes
—drugs and dance
and sex—always sex
—sometimes mistaken for love
a freak of games
playing by somebody else's rules
before she knew how

a freak of secret dreams
that should have long since happened
to be one who started
playing a little too late
and one who was old
before she was young
for when she was young
oh, how she wanted to
change the world back then

alas, when she was older
oh, how she wanted to lock
the world out…

she, the freak, who was
mommy's little girl
was taught all the right things
had all the right toys

what happened?
her mother wondered

she, the freak, was always seeking love
until her hair was white

oh, Lord
until her hair was white

her mother warned her to be careful
her father, he didn't care at all

for she was a fool to him—
always the fool

she, the freak, can really help change
the world
for she has the mind and heart to do so

but, oh, if only she could capture love
to help her make up
for the time when she
was old before she was young
alas, she was too old to be young

Dear God, what happened to all the toys?
No, she, the freak, never found her place
for she was both young and old

she was old before her time
when youth urged to be cherished
and when she wanted to play

My God, where had all the time gone?
It ran out, m' dear...
time simply ran out...

HAUNTINGS

Some things linger on my mind, mainly through stories that I have heard. A friend of mine told me about a murder that she saw in broad daylight while looking out of her window. She saw a group of young men surrounding a young man who cried out, "I thought we were family!" then "Oh my god! They cut my heart!"

This young man was being stabbed to death during the day on Magnolia Street right off Springfield Avenue. My friend told me that she had called the cops, but they never came. Perhaps this is due to her word phrasing. She told the operator that there was a fight. She stated that she kept looking and waited for the cops to come. In the meantime, the group picked up the poor young man and took him inside their building. She then said that they brought him back out when it was dark and threw him in the trunk of a car.

Approximately two weeks after she told me this, I heard on the local radio station, WWNJR, that the police were trying to solve a murder of a young man who was found in an empty lot and had been stabbed numerous times. The body was found on Eighteenth Avenue just down the street from Magnolia and Springfield Avenue. Now that I think about it, why didn't I do or say something? That may have been the young man my friend was telling me about.

Nowadays, murder is so common; it's an everyday occurrence. It's so sad to see and hear about all these young men killing one another in the streets of Newark, New Jersey. This story haunts me because I remember his last words, "I thought we were family." So many young black men had to grow up in the system (foster care) without any ties to their blood family. They grow up being placed from home to home in the foster care system just to be released at the age of eighteen with no post support system. They have nowhere to go and no one to turn to.

Finding people that you bond with and relate to as family can be a blessing because you finally belong somewhere. You have found your home and family. Isn't that the dream of every foster child? But to be betrayed as this slain young man was, his idea of family was killing him. Metaphorically speaking, not only was this young man's heart cut, but it was also broken at the same time. This young man died with a broken heart, and I can't think of anything worse than that. Can you? I am haunted by the knowledge that this happened to this young man.

I remember one day, dropping off my granddaughter at Whitman Street school when she was in kindergarten, I saw this little boy who was always fighting and getting into trouble being dropped off by his mother in the lobby. It appeared as if the little boy was confused and didn't know which way to go. The sad truth of it is that he may have been so high off of Ritalin that he couldn't focus. Sadly, the school system in Newark creates drug addicts. If a child has issues that cannot be controlled, they are recommended to go to Beth Israel Hospital for an assessment. They cannot return back to school unless they are assessed. So they go to Beth Israel and are assessed with a disorder that required Ritalin.

I attended Rutgers University graduate school for social work. We had to do our fieldwork, and one of my classmates was assigned to Beth Israel. She and I were discussing the school system and Ritalin. As a matter of fact, she told me that the LCSW who did the assessments at Beth Israel at the time always diagnosed every child who walked in the doors with some disorder, never minding the extenuating circumstances.

Now, let's do the math. A child is recommended for an assessment. It's set up with the city and school system whether the child gets a free assessment at Beth Israel Hospital. The child is assessed as having some type of disorder, and Ritalin is the popular drug at the time. I believe *20/20* did a special on Ritalin about how potent it was. That it is comparable to heroin and makes the user predisposed to drug use. Now can you just imagine how many dreams were terminated? Sad, isn't it? No wonder I stayed in my room and just wrote during those first years of living in Newark, New Jersey.

POEM

How far can a bird fly?

As high—as high—
as he desires

How far can the eagle soar?

As far—as far—
as he wills

How far can I go?
I don't know—don't know

DEATH OF A MUSICIAN (PIED PIPER)

And finally when all the music inside of him was spent—
He closed his eyes for a final sleep.

Reflections

Life: According to Mrs. Callie Mae Haskins

Callie Mae Haskins walks out of her first-floor apartment. She is proudly wearing her "ten-gallon" white cowboy hat and totin' her shiny brown enameled cane with metal medallions attached to it from the very top to the very bottom. Callie bravely works her way toward the drug store, which is two blocks away. The drug store is the local meeting spot for all the seniors in the surrounding area. Callie Mae lives in a senior complex located in Falls Church, Virginia.

Callie Mae is ninety-seven years old. However, she has proclaimed to have reached the age of one hundred years old ten years ago for reasons unknown. Once she did try to explain to me why she was in the local paper celebrating her one-hundredth birthday. Unfortunately, I was too self-involved and thinking about my boyfriend and passionately smoking a cigarette. I regret that I never actually took the time to listen to her sometimes. I am ashamed. However, I did manage to catch the words, "I had to say that." Reflecting back, I really, really regret the fact that I did not take the time out to listen to all that she had to say. Now I wonder what pressure was she under that would make her feel obligated to exaggerate her birthday? I feel bad about not listening to that day. Now I can see the struggle that Callie Mae has gone through. I admire and respect her for the fact that she's simply survived life this long. She'd held tightly onto a life that was not often kind to her.

Callie Mae was the oldest of eleven children. She is the only result of her mother's first marriage to a "100-percent Cherokee-blooded man" who died at an early age of tuberculosis. Callie Mae was born in North Carolina, and she's always insisted that she's not Black. She would say to me over and over again, "Honey, I'm not black. My mother was white and Indian. My father was all Indian."

When I first heard this, I went into a state of shock! I wondered why was it that I had a grandmother who wasn't black? I'm black, and I always looked upon her as being black. I considered her to be a light-skinned black woman because I'm light-skinned also. But to hear her say that she wasn't black just blew my mind. I thought that she was in denial at first, but when she "broke it down," I had to admit that the old gal wasn't black. She is basically a Native American with a dab of whiteness in her. However, if you saw her, you would mistake her for a little old "white lady." When she starts talking about her "good white friends," you know immediately that she is not white. The reason she emphasizes her "white friends" is some crazy form of social status according to some elderly southern blacks. Having "white friends" is a social mobility mechanism, which places you on a higher plane in the social hierarchy.

Now the reason why Callie Mae emphasizes that she's not black is another survival tool. I can see that now as I write this paper. During her lifetime, the color line was very important. It was especially important in the south where Callie Mae grew up. Sometimes, life was a little bit easier on poor blacks if they looked almost white. The whites were still mean and hateful. Yet at times, not as hateful toward lighter-skinned blacks. The rule was that the lighter, the better, and Callie Mae declares that she was among the lightest. She wasn't even black. Unfortunately, although not being black, Callie Mae still grew up black, which meant a life of poverty and racism. It meant being called a nigger, which meant that she was black, inferior, and worthless in the eyes of the people she called "good white friends." Yes, Callie Mae grew up black, and she felt the pain that comes along with being black. Her mother remarried a black man, and Callie Mae's brothers and sisters were considered black.

Although most of them were very light-skinned with long, curly hair, according to Grandma Callie, her stepfather was cruel and treated her badly. Callie Mae wasn't given special privileges as her siblings. She was forced to become a surrogate mother to her siblings.

She wasn't allowed to be a child. She became a substitute mother to her sister Lucy when she was five. Her childhood ended at age five. Her struggle in life appeared to have started at five years old.

Eventually, Callie Mae grew up and, at the age of seventeen, married Taft Haskins, who was my grandfather. Taft was a tall, powerful black man with a very, very loud voice. I remember this because it seemed as if he was always shouting when he talked, but he wasn't. Grandma Callie never said anything bad about Grandpa Tad even though when they were divorced. However, my uncle Junior (the baby) has pointed out that Grandpa was a wife-beater and child abuser. Junior has stated, "Your grandpa was the meanest man out here." Also, Junior has said other things, implying that there's a lot more to Grandpa Tad than meets the eye.

If this were true, I can now see the brave front that my grandmother, Callie, has put up all these years. Also, I can see that she fell into a cycle of abuse. First, from her stepfather; secondly, from her husband, which is a pattern typical for abused female children. None of my other aunts and uncles or mother has ever mentioned being abused. However, back in those days, it was called "a good-ole butt whipping." Parents would beat their children's behind until they were too sore to sit down. I know. I've felt the blows.

You see, this tradition was passed down to my mother. It worked because whatever you did to deserve that beating, you made sure that you never did it again. Nowadays, everything is considered child abuse. This is something that my grandmother, Callie, cannot understand. She has proclaimed that she used to "tear those tails up." Together, Taft and Callie Mae had ten children: Cubbie, Bryce, Henry, Jimmy, Harold, Junior, Sister, Priscilla, Ann, and my mother, Phyllis.

Tragedy and a black cloud hung over Callie Mae's children. Due to the time period and location in which they were born, their life chances were slim. They grew up in the 1930s and 1940s. The Haskin children, along with their peers, had to walk miles down the road to a one-room schoolhouse, which was located at Saint Mark Baptist Church in Buffalo Junction, Virginia. Due to circumstances, it was hard for the children to go to school because sometimes they had no shoes to wear, or they had to work in the fields with their father. Therefore, education was not easily attainable for them in rural Virginia. Consequently, the older boys left and moved to northern Virginia in search of work. Harold, at the age of twenty-one, was tragically killed in a construction accident. Later, Jimmy died of complications from a broken jaw.

The girls married young. Sister, who was the oldest girl, died suddenly in a house fire. She was seven months pregnant and seventeen years old. Ann, who Grandma Callie says was very, very pretty, married a local alcoholic named William Terry. According to Grandma Callie, William transformed pretty Aunt Ann into an alcoholic also. Unfortunately, I don't remember Aunt Ann ever being pretty, but she did have the deepest dimples on the side of both of her cheeks when she smiled. Phyllis, married at fifteen, was pregnant with me, to a man twenty-four years older than her. He was my father, Richard Yancey. Priscilla and Junior were the only ones who graduated from high school. This is because they are the babies of the family. They became school-age after Grandma Callie moved to the city. There is almost a twenty-year gap between them and the oldest child, Cubbie, who was deceased.

Callie Mae has lived to see five of her children pass on before her. This is something that I find amazing about my grandmother. Losing a child is one of the worst things that can happen to anyone. Yet she's gone through this ordeal several times, and she survived. My grandmother talks to God all the time. She always starts with, "Well, Father," then she'll add on what else she wants to talk to God about. The main thing that I've learned from my grandmother is that she always puts God first. God is her strength and her salvation. I admire and respect this trait in her so much. Watching her gives me the strength to face my life and go on.

One day, while we were sitting around in Grandma Callie's apartment, she told me the story about, "Tiny." Tiny is my dead aunt, Sister's baby. She is the baby that my aunt was pregnant with when she was burned. Tiny survived, and she came into this world. Grandma Callie has always said that God has a reason for everything. Tiny's life is a miracle by itself. She was born prematurely and blind. The doctors said that she wouldn't make it. When she was a little over three months old, Uncle Ralph (Tiny's father) gave Tiny to Grandma Callie to take care of.

Grandma Callie said that she used to just let Tiny lay in the sun to heal her. You see, old people from the South know how to heal. This is just something that is passed on from generation to generation. Grandma Callie wasn't formally educated at all. She can't read or write, but she can sign her name. However, she's educated in other ways that are more valuable than formal education. Grandma Callie doesn't know the specifics about vitamin D being in the rays of the sun. But she does know the healing effects of the sun, which she gives credit to her mother, who was basically a Native American.

Native Americans are a holistic people. The healing of Tiny was a godly and cultural phenomenon. Grandma Callie used prayer and the knowledge that she knew to help heal Tiny. God heard Grandma Callie's prayers and healed her grandchild. The doctor said that Tiny wouldn't make it, but Grandma Callie prayed that she would be healed—and it was done.

This is another thing that truly amazes me about Granma Callie. She pays no attention to what men say. She completely puts her faith in God and prayer. Because of her, I can proudly say that I come from a praying family. When I go visit her, especially on her birthday, which is Christmas, the whole family gets together; and before it's all over, a prayer circle has been formed. Now Grandma Callie, as a lot of old people from the south, talks about spirits and things like that, which is why I don't sleep in the dark.

Once, Grandma Callie told me about her seeing Uncle Bryce (after he died) getting some iced tea out of the refrigerator. This is because he loved her iced tea. I simply asked, "Are you serious?"

She responded quite seriously, "Yes, child, ask Junior."

This is because Junior is the family spiritualist who knows about that stuff. Grandma Callie said this is because Junior was born with a veil over his eyes. The veil is supposed to allow a child to have a gift of prophecy. Well, I don't know about all that. However, I must admit that when I ask Junior something, most times, his answers turn out to be true. Spooky!

Callie Mae Haskins is one of the most interesting people that I know. There is a deep history to her life, which is also my history, and I learn about my roots from her. She has led a very unusual and blessed life. She has survived a cold world that really had no place for her. She grew up in the segregated South when the Jim Crow laws were in full effect. She earned money for her family by cleaning white people's houses, houses that had to be entered the back way because she was not allowed to go through the front door. She cleaned their toilets, cooked their meals, and washed and ironed their clothes. She helped raise their children.

Callie Mae is a survivor, and she still manages to smile. Her smile is covered with a brown substance called "dipping snuff." She says that she's been dipping snuff her whole life. She's even told me that Grandpa Tad is the only man who ever kissed her. Well, I definitely believe that! Grandma Callie is a trip! Through talking and just by being around Granma Callie, I have learned the life lesson of strength and perseverance which is due to a strong faith in God.

All this has been demonstrated to me by Grandma Callie. So I can understand why she wears that big old white cowboy hat. It's her crown of glory. I can understand why she has metals affixed to her cane. They are her medals of honor. "Go ahead, and strut your stuff, Miss Callie Mae! You deserve it."

ABOUT THE AUTHOR

Marian Yancey was born on December 31, 1957, in her grand-mother's house with the assistance of a midwife, Emma Yancey, who was her father's first cousin. During the first thirteen years of her life, she grew up and stayed on the family farm. She lived in the very house that she was born in for those first thirteen years of her life. She lived and grew up in a very isolated world. Tragically, she had to move from the peaceful, isolated world of her grandmother's home and farm to the total opposite of what she was used to. She was moved to Newark, New Jersey. She had to adjust to her new environment, and she always wondered why the kids in her new school were so small and dirty looking. Why didn't they brush their teeth? These questions affected her life. She would go on to major in sociology and social science to understand her new environment.